I0410998

STAKEHOLDER
REPORT 2010

DEFENSE SECURITY SERVICE

MESSAGE FROM DSS DIRECTOR

I'm pleased to provide the second Stakeholder Report of the Defense Security Service (DSS). We launched the first report in response to lingering questions about the DSS mission and status. I think we've finally convinced the community that we're no longer in the personnel security investigation business. I think we have also demonstrated that DSS has turned a corner and is stable and well-positioned to meet the demands of our Stakeholders – both within the government and in industry.

To meet these demands however, DSS cannot rest on its laurels, but must continue to look at ways to improve its internal operations and satisfy the needs of the community. This document articulates our new focus in Counterintelligence on building a culture of "catching spies." It also recognizes that a comprehensive cyber security strategy is absolutely critical to protecting and defending industry and the Department against cyber intrusions. Delivering on-demand training is no longer a luxury, but an operational requirement for the DSS Academy. Internally, DSS continues to refine its staff assistance and quality assurance processes to ensure a unified, consistent process is communicated to the industrial base, and IT solutions provide efficiencies across the agency.

It's an exciting time to be at DSS. We have much to be proud of, but much to do to continue to deliver the world class service we have committed to provide. Thank you for reading and your continued support of DSS.

Kathleen M. Watson
Director

VISION

DSS is the premier provider of industrial security services in the Department of Defense (DoD), improving the security of our nation and its warfighters.

A PROFESSIONAL AND FULLY INTEGRATED AND SEAMLESS ENTERPRISE, PROVIDING THE BEST INTELLIGENCE, COUNTERINTELLIGENCE, AND SECURITY UNDER ANY CONDITION OR CIRCUMSTANCE, WHENEVER AND WHEREVER, IN SUPPORT OF THE WAR FIGHTER AND THE NATION.

VISION OF THE DEFENSE INTELLIGENCE ENTERPRISE

DEFENSE INTELLIGENCE STRATEGY, 2008
SECRETARY OF DEFENSE ROBERT M. GATES

MISSION

DSS supports national security and the warfighter, secures the nation's technological base, and oversees the protection of U.S. and foreign classified information in the hands of industry under the National Industrial Security Program (NISP) – on behalf of the Department of Defense and 23 other Federal Agencies that have signed agreements with the Secretary of Defense.

We accomplish this mission by performing six mission essential tasks:

- Clear industrial facilities, personnel and associated information systems.
- Identify unlawful penetrators of the defense industrial base.
- Manage foreign ownership, control and influence (FOCI) in cleared industry.
- Provide advice and oversight to industry.
- Deliver security education and training.
- Provide critical mission support operations.

WE MUST KEEP OUR EYE FIXED ON THE WORLD WE SEEK TO BUILD — ONE THAT DEFEATS OUR ADVERSARIES, BUT THAT ALSO PROMOTES DIGNITY AND OPPORTUNITY AND JUSTICE FOR ALL WHO STAND WITH US. TO DO THAT, WE NEED YOU TO KEEP STANDING AND SERVING TOGETHER — EVERY AGENCY, EVERY DEPARTMENT, EVERY BRANCH, EVERY LEVEL. ONE TEAM. ONE MISSION. THAT'S HOW WE'RE GOING TO PREVAIL IN THIS FIGHT, AND THAT'S HOW WE'RE GOING TO PROTECT THIS COUNTRY THAT WE ALL LOVE.

BARACK H. OBAMA
PRESIDENT OF THE UNITED STATES

DSS SEAL

The three divisions of the shield refer to the three basic requirements of all investigations: patient inquiry, observation, and careful examination of the facts.

The eagle, adopted from that used in the seal of DoD, alludes to keenness of vision, strength, and tenacity that symbolizes DSS.

The three arrows, also adopted from the seal of DoD, refer to the Armed Services, comprising the military components of DSS. In crossing over and protectively covering the Pentagon, these arrows represent the DoD wide aspects of the DSS mission.

The color dark blue, the National color, represents the United States, and the color light blue represents DoD, the shade of blue being used by the Defense Department. The pattern indicates the integral unity of the United States, DoD, and DSS. The color gold (or yellow) is symbolic of zeal and achievement.

On a white disc within a border of blue with gold outer rim is the shield of DSS in full color blazoned above a wreath of laurel and olive proper (as depicted on the DoD seal). Inscribed at top of the white disc is "Defense Security Service" and in the base, in smaller letters, is "United States of America," all letters gold.

The laurel and olives symbolizes merit and peace; the color white signifies "deeds worthy of remembrance."

ORGANIZATIONAL OVERVIEW

Command Elements

Office of the Chief Financial Officer	Executive Steering Committee & Stakeholders Board			Office of Aquisitions
Office of the General Counsel	Director & Chair			Office of Legislative Affairs
Office of the Inspector General	Deputy Director & Vice Chair	Chief Financial Officer	Chief of Staff	Office of Public Affairs
Equal Employment Opportunity	Deputy Chief of Staff	Director, CI	Director, IO	Base Realignment and Closure (BRAC)
	Director, SETA	Director, IP	Chief Information Officer	

Operational Elements

Counterintelligence (CI)	Industrial Security Field Operations (IO)	Security Education Training & Awareness (SETA)	Industrial Policy & Programs (IP)

Enabling Elements

Comptroller & Financial Management Division	Support Services Division	Office of Human Resourcees & Security	Office of the Chief Information Officer (OCIO)

HISTORY

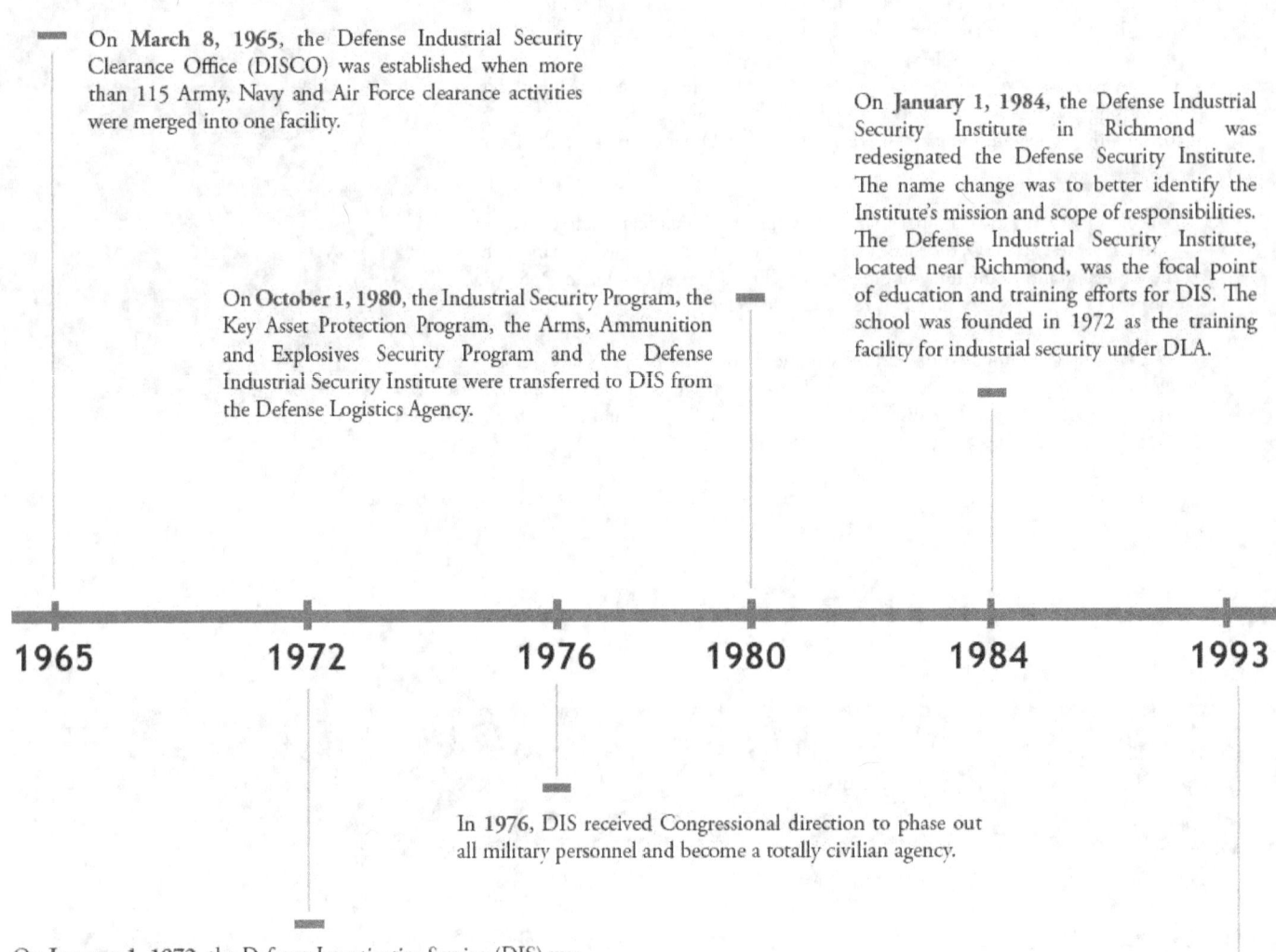

On **March 8, 1965**, the Defense Industrial Security Clearance Office (DISCO) was established when more than 115 Army, Navy and Air Force clearance activities were merged into one facility.

On **October 1, 1980**, the Industrial Security Program, the Key Asset Protection Program, the Arms, Ammunition and Explosives Security Program and the Defense Industrial Security Institute were transferred to DIS from the Defense Logistics Agency.

On **January 1, 1984**, the Defense Industrial Security Institute in Richmond was redesignated the Defense Security Institute. The name change was to better identify the Institute's mission and scope of responsibilities. The Defense Industrial Security Institute, located near Richmond, was the focal point of education and training efforts for DIS. The school was founded in 1972 as the training facility for industrial security under DLA.

1965   1972   1976   1980   1984   1993

In **1976**, DIS received Congressional direction to phase out all military personnel and become a totally civilian agency.

On **January 1, 1972**, the Defense Investigative Service (DIS) was established. DIS was created in response to President Richard M. Nixon's approval of proposals suggesting the reorganization of the national intelligence community and the creation of an "Office of Defense Investigation" to consolidate Department of Defense (DoD) personnel security investigations (PSI). Prior to this consolidation, such work was accomplished through the U.S. military departments by four major DoD investigative agencies. They were: 1) the U.S. Army Intelligence Command, 2) the U.S. Army Criminal Investigative Command, 3) the Naval Investigative Service, and 4) the Office of Special Investigations, Air Force.

On **January 6, 1993**, President George W. Bush signed Executive Order 12829, that established the National Industrial Security Program. This program was intended to replace not only the DISP, but the industrial security programs of the Central Intelligence Agency, the Department of Energy and the Nuclear Regulatory Commission.

In **May 1993**, DIS established a counterintelligence (CI) office.

On **April 1, 1995**, the National Industrial Security Program Operating Manual (NISPOM) became effective, formally implementing the National Industrial Security Program. It was the most significant change in the Industrial Security Program in nearly 40 years.

On **April 19, 1995**, the Alfred P. Murrah Building in Oklahoma City was bombed, killing DIS employees Bob Westberry, Larry Cottingham, Peter DeMaster, Jean Johnson and Larry Turner in the Oklahoma City Investigative Field Office. DIS dedicated two living memorials to them – an Oklahoma Red Bud Tree at the Headquarters building and a cherry tree by the Tidal Basin.

On **February 4, 2003**, the Commission of the Council on Occupational Education (COE), a national accrediting authority recognized by the Department of Education, granted accreditation to the Defense Security Service Academy. This award of accreditation was based on COE's evaluation that the Academy met not only the standards of quality of the Commission, but also the needs of its students and community. The DSS Academy was reaccredited in 2009.

On **December 18, 2007**, the Director of DSS was named the functional manager for DoD Security Training.

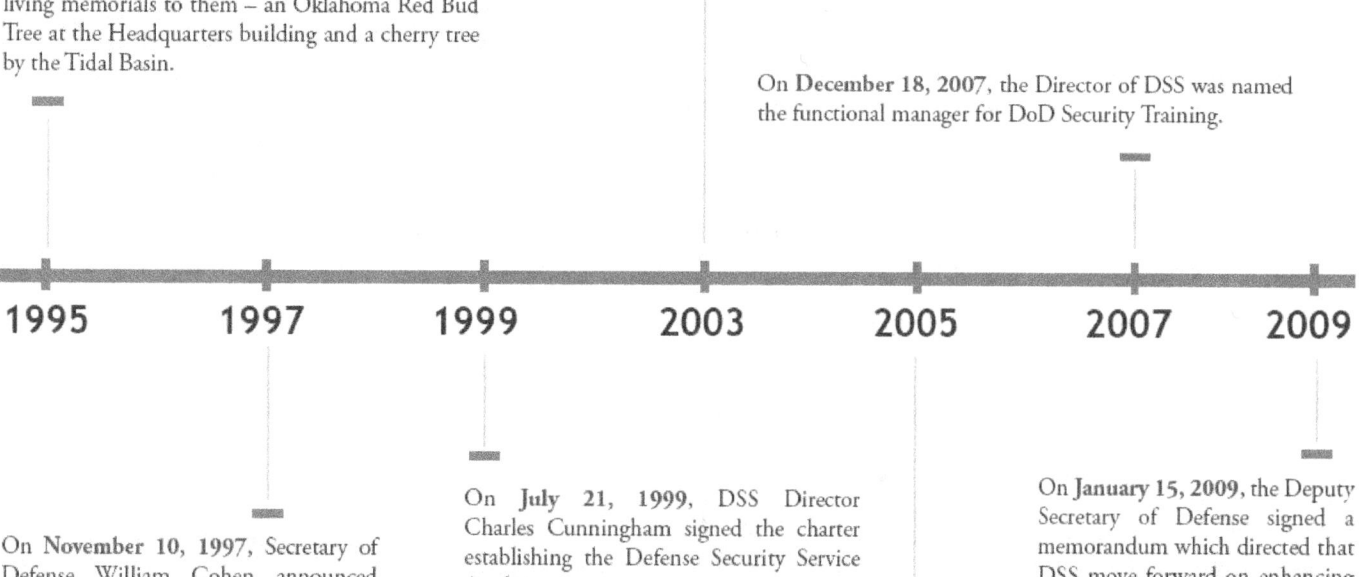

1995   1997   1999   2003   2005   2007   2009

On **November 10, 1997**, Secretary of Defense William Cohen announced that DIS would be redesignated as the Defense Security Service. The name change was effective **November 25, 1997**. The Department made the change to reflect the agency's broader mission and functions.

On **July 21, 1999**, DSS Director Charles Cunningham signed the charter establishing the Defense Security Service Academy.

On **January 15, 2009**, the Deputy Secretary of Defense signed a memorandum which directed that DSS move forward on enhancing the National Industrial Security Program and reinvigorating the Security Education Training and Awareness Program, in an effort to "strengthen and refocus DSS to meet 21st century industrial security and counterintelligence needs."

On **February 20, 2005**, DSS transferred the personnel security investigations function to the Office of Personnel Management. This included PSIs for industry personnel under the National Industrial Security Program (NISP) and the transfer of approximately 1,850 personnel. DSS retained the function, on behalf of DoD, to oversee the OPM billing and financial reconciliation process for PSIs for the entire Department.

INDUSTRIAL SECURITY FIELD OPERATIONS

Industrial Security Field Operations (IO) inspects and provides oversight to cleared defense industry on behalf of DoD and 23 National Industrial Security Program partners.

270 Industrial Security Representatives spread across the United States

- Provide advice and assistance
- Inspect facilities for compliance with established guidelines
- Report security incidents and provide remediation

83 Information System Security Professionals (ISSP) provide integrated support

- Provide technical expertise to identify key threats facing industry today
- Certify and accredit industry information systems

Adjudicate clearances for contractors (DISCO)

Facts:

- 13,036 active, cleared facilities in NISP; (9,712 cleared business families)
- 9,225 facility security inspections (FY09)
- 1,650 new facility clearances granted (FY09)
    - o   970 facility clearances terminated for a net increase of 680 active, cleared facilities (FY09)
- 14,355 accredited IT systems in industry
- Average time for system accreditation: 32.5 days

Adjudicate Industry Security Clearances

- More than 1.1M active cleared contractors
- 298,489 Personnel Security Adjudication actions (FY09)
    - o   161,018 final eligibility decisions
    - o   118,323 interim decisions
- Met the IRTPA* goal of 20 days average to adjudicate all initial clearances

Intelligence Reform and Terrorism Prevention Act of 2004 mandated specific goals for improving timelines for both personnel security investigations and adjudications.

IDENTIFY, DENY, DISRUPT AND EXPLOIT FOREIGN INTELLIGENCE AND SECURITY SERVICE ACTIVITIES TARGETING THOSE INTERESTS AND SHARE INFORMATION WITH NATIONAL-LEVEL PARTNERS. SUPPORT THE PROTECTION OF U.S. DEPARTMENT OF DEFENSE PERSONNEL, FACILITIES, TECHNOLOGIES, SOURCES AND METHODS.

DEFENSE INTELLIGENCE STRATEGY, 2008

U.S. MAP WITH DSS LOCATIONS

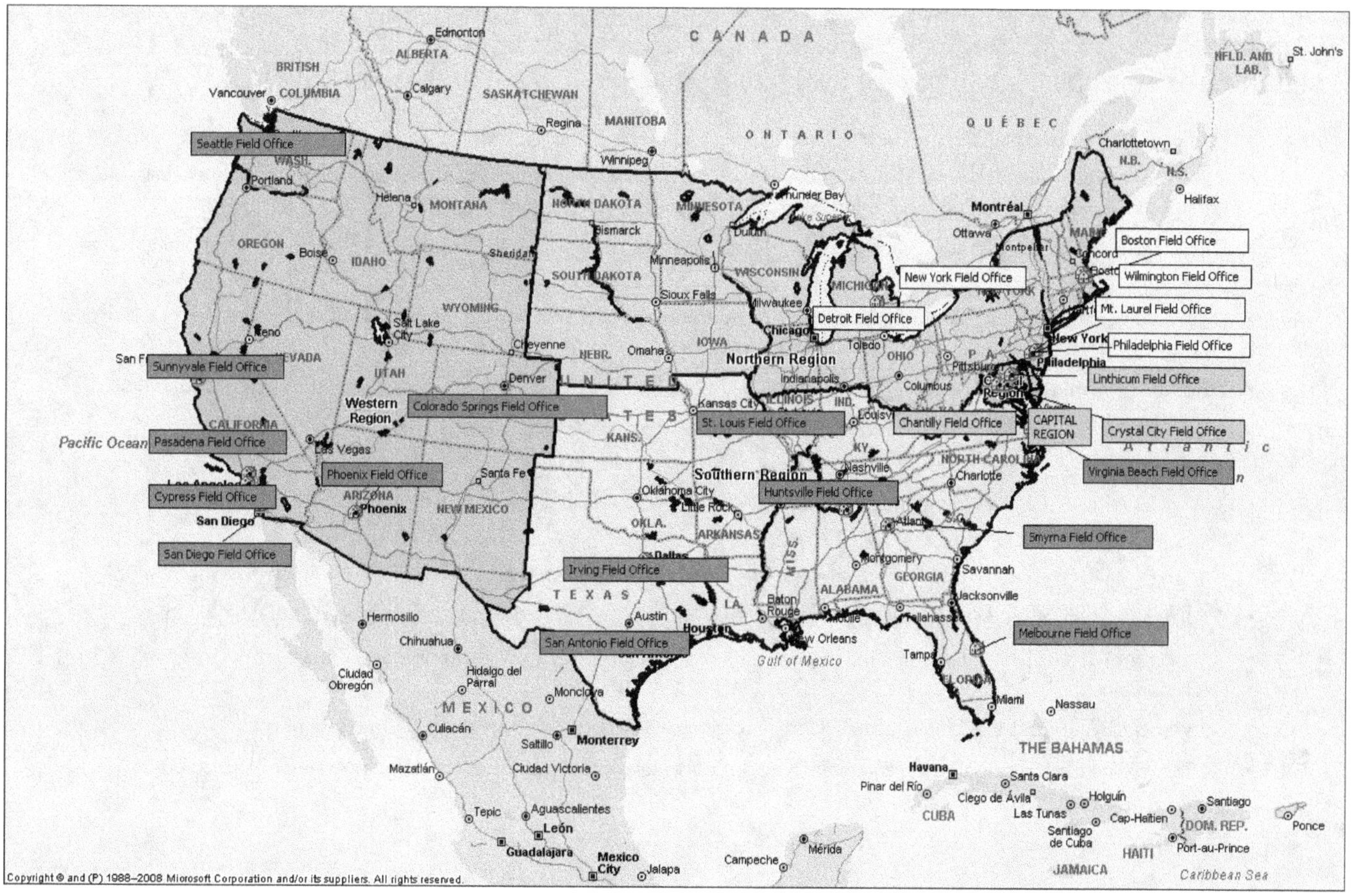

Capital Region, Arlington, VA
Bryans Road, MD
Fort Meade, MD (under BRAC)
Lexington Park, MD
Linthicum, MD
Arlington, VA
Chantilly, VA
Fredericksburg, VA
Quantico, VA (under BRAC)

Northern Region, Boston, MA
Groton, CT
Shelton, CT
Andover, MA
Boston, MA
Wilmington, MA
Detroit, MI
Livonia, MI
Fort Snelling, MN
Mt. Laurel, NJ
Picatinny Arsenal, NJ
Syracuse-Liverpool, NY
Watervliet-Arsenal, NY
Westbury, NY
Williamsville, NY
Cincinnati, OH
Cleveland, OH
Wright-Patterson AFB, OH
Fort Indiantown Gap, PA
Lester, PA
McClure, PA
Philadelphia, PA
Sewickley, PA
Milwaukee, WI

Southern Region, Irving, TX
Huntsville, AL
Homestead, FL
Hurlburt Field, FL
Jacksonville, FL
Melbourne, FL
Orlando, FL
Tampa, FL
Smyrna, GA
Des Plaines, IL
Downers Grove, IL
Indianapolis, IN
Kansas City, KS
Slidell, LA
St. Louis, MO
Gulfport, MS
Charlotte, NC
Raleigh, NC
Offutt Air Force Base, NE
Oklahoma City, OK
Charleston, SC
San Antonio, TX
El Paso, TX
Irving, TX
Hampton, VA
Virginia Beach, VA

Western Region, San Diego, CA
Anchorage, AK
Phoenix, AZ
Tucson, AZ
Camarillo, CA
Cypress, CA
Dublin, CA
Encino, CA
Palmdale, CA
Pasadena, CA
San Diego, CA
Santa Barbara, CA
Sunnyvale, CA
Travis Air Force Base, CA
Colorado Springs, CO
Denver, CO
Honolulu, HI
Albuquerque, NM
Seattle, WA
Bountiful, UT

7

COUNTERINTELLIGENCE

Counterintelligence (CI) identifies "unlawful penetrators" who illicitly attempt to obtain DoD information and technologies resident in the cleared Defense Industrial Base. DSS CI Specialists work in partnership with industry and other DSS partners to:

- Determine hostile involvement, identify intelligence collection trends and provide a baseline for effective countermeasures to protect classified technology and programs at risk for foreign or hostile targeting;
- Leverage national counterintelligence and federal law enforcement resources to effectively neutralize or exploit penetration attempts;
- Communicate lessons learned through an aggressive education and awareness program to help industry become the CI "First Line of Defense" against a pervasive and growing threat; and
- Encourage an enhanced Insider Threat program focusing on building a "culture of catching spies" within the cleared contractor community.

Facts:

- 45 individuals or entities under investigation as possible "unlawful penetrators" based on DSS CI developed information
- 6 federal law enforcement agencies conducting investigations or operations as a result of referrals from DSS CI
- 11 confirmed incidents of foreign intelligence and security services involvement in collection attempts targeting key technologies
- 165 incidents of "probable" foreign Intelligence and security services involvement in collection attempts
- 1489 reports where foreign intelligence and security services involvement in collection attempts cannot be ruled out

WE ARE ENTERING AN ERA MARKED BY PACE, SCOPE AND COMPLEXITY OF CHANGE THAT WILL CHALLENGE THE MINDS AND RESOURCES OF THE DEFENSE INTELLIGENCE ENTERPRISE. THE CHALLENGE TO PROVIDE THE INFORMATION, INSIGHT AND WARNING THAT ALLOW OUR NATIONAL MILITARY AND CIVILIAN LEADERS TO MAKE BETTER DECISIONS BOTH IN WASHINGTON AND ON THE FIELD OF BATTLE HAS NEVER BEEN GREATER OR MORE URGENT. IT WILL REQUIRE A CONCERTED, COLLECTIVE EFFORT BY THE DEPARTMENT OF DEFENSE INTELLIGENCE, COUNTERINTELLIGENCE AND SECURITY COMMUNITIES TO PROTECT OUR MILITARY AND INTELLIGENCE ASSETS AGAINST ALL FORMS AND DOMAINS OF ATTACK AND TRANSFORM THE DEFENSE INTELLIGENCE ENTERPRISE INTO ONE THAT IS AGILE, GLOBAL AND DIVERSE.

JAMES R. CLAPPER
UNDER SECRETARY OF DEFENSE (INTELLIGENCE)

DEFENSE INTELLIGENCE STRATEGY, 2008

INDUSTRIAL POLICY AND PROGRAMS

Industrial Policy and Programs (IP) supports the National Industrial Security Program:

- Mitigate foreign ownership, control or influence (FOCI)
- Implement FOCI mitigation agreements
- Administer international programs
- Issue internal DSS policies and procedures
- Interpret industrial and personnel security policies
- Develop projections for industry personnel security investigations
- Provide analytic support

Facts:

- 620 FOCI facilities
- 249 FOCI mitigation agreements
- Support to 65 foreign countries

NISP PSI Projections:

- Industry PSI submissions were 97.6 percent of the projected 182,315 cases
- Over $215 million expended overall in FY09

ATTACKS ARE ON THE RISE AGAINST OUR DEFENSE CONTRACTORS, WHO
FACE CYBER ESPIONAGE FROM FOREIGN GOVERNMENTS, COMPETITORS
AND CRIMINALS. INDEED, MAJOR AEROSPACE WEAPONS PLATFORMS HAVE
EXPERIENCED INTRUSIONS THAT HAVE COMPROMISED UNCLASSIFIED
BUT SENSITIVE TECHNICAL INFORMATION.

WILLIAM J. LYNN III
DEPUTY SECRETARY OF DEFENSE

SECURITY EDUCATION, TRAINING AND AWARENESS (SETA)

SETA delivers security education and training to DoD and the cleared contractor community through formal classroom, web-based and correspondence/distance learning. Over the past year, in order to meet the demand by security professionals for "the right content, for the right person, at the right time, and in the right place," SETA has continued its efforts to move from a classroom-based environment to a web-based delivery platform. DSS, with assistance from the DoD Security Training Council, has developed the DoD Security Skill Standards. These standards serve as the foundation for the DoD Security Certification Program currently under development. The first level of the Security Certification Program is scheduled for implementation in the fourth quarter of FY10.

Facts:

- Trained 79,897 students trained in FY09 (Represents a 49 percent increase over FY08)
- Deployed 27 new courses in FY09
- Developing 33 courses at request of stakeholders
- Deployed seven new security information/job aid videos
- Developing two additional security information/job aid videos
- Participated in 23 security forums and conferences, with approximately 4,000 personnel in attendance, providing overviews of SETA highlighting training opportunities and providing guidance to security professionals in attendance.
- Chair the Department of Defense Security Training Council (DSTC) -- the advisory body representing the DoD security training community.

OUR MISSION IS A FULLY INTEGRATED INTELLIGENCE COMMUNITY, AND THERE IS NO TURNING BACK. MY MOST URGENT PRIORITIES ARE TO PERMANENTLY INSTILL THIS NEW CULTURE AND TO USE EVERY TOOL AT MY DISPOSAL — FROM JOINT DUTY TO RECRUITMENT AND COMMUNICATIONS — TO BUILD A GENERATION OF INTELLIGENCE LEADERS FOR WHOM THIS CULTURE IS BUSINESS AS USUAL.

DENNIS C. BLAIR
DIRECTOR OF NATIONAL INTELLIGENCE

CHIEF INFORMATION OFFICER

The Office of Chief Information Officer (OCIO) works closely with DSS leadership to ensure that information technology systems continually meet mission requirements. Current focus areas include:

- Classified and unclassified network connectivity
- Legacy system sustainment, office automation and web services
- Dual Call Center management
- Information assurance/computer network defense
- New systems and application development

The OCIO manages and maintains the Enterprise Security Systems (ESS) in support of the industrial security and personnel security missions which support over 100,000 users world-wide. These legacy Information Technology Systems, such as the Joint Personnel Adjudication System (JPAS), will transition to the Defense Manpower Data Center in FY10 at the direction of the Deputy Secretary of Defense.

THE CYBER SECURITY CHALLENGES WE FACE EVERY DAY AT THE DEFENSE DEPARTMENT—ALBEIT ON A VERY MUCH LARGER SCALE THAN SOME—ARE NOT UNLIKE THOSE FACED BY YOUR AGENCIES, YOUR INDUSTRIES, YOUR INSTITUTIONS. THERE'S NO EXAGGERATING OUR DEPENDENCE ON OUR INFORMATION NETWORKS—IN OUR CASE, A 21ST CENTURY MILITARY THAT SIMPLY CANNOT FUNCTION WITHOUT THEM. AND THERE'S NO EXAGGERATING THE THREAT. IT'S UNPRECEDENTED IN ITS SOURCE, ITS SPEED AND ITS SCOPE.

WILLIAM J. LYNN III
DEPUTY SECRETARY OF DEFENSE

ACHIEVEMENTS AND CASE STUDIES

DSS continually assesses its oversight of the industrial security program to ensure the most robust mechanisms for the protection of classified information in industry are in place. During the past year DSS has launched a number of new initiatives in support of its mission.

NEW INITIATIVES

Cyber Security

DSS is developing an agency-wide cyber security strategy to ensure that cyber security is fully integrated into the DSS industrial security mission. The strategy identifies the activities necessary for DSS to fund, organize, equip, and staff its headquarters and train its field offices to operate as a single integrated team for cyber security: field operations, counterintelligence, policy and programs, information technology and support activities.

DSS has placed employees at the Defense Cyber Crime Center and the National Cyber Investigative Joint Task Force to ensure DSS is fully integrated into the community effort addressing this threat.

As a result of these efforts, DSS is better positioned to ensure that cyber threats to cleared industry and ultimately the Department of Defense are mitigated to preclude the loss or compromise of classified information.

Staff Assistance Visits

In 2008 and 2009, DSS established and conducted its first Field Office Staff Assistance Visits (SAV). The SAV is a quality assurance program designed to continuously assess and monitor field office operations. The goal of SAV is to gain insight into the status of field operations, identify areas for improvement, and identify best practice processes and procedures that can be shared and adopted among field offices. DSS has also hired a Quality Assurance Manager who will oversee the SAV process and develop a quality assurance program in FY10.

Adopting and internalizing the SAV process provides several benefits to DSS. Regional Directors and Field Office Chiefs have better tools to manage their operations and a codified procedure to share and learn from one another. Adopting best practices and processes will also lead to more consistent operations across the agency's field operations.

FOCI analytic products

The Foreign Ownership Control or Influence (FOCI) Analytic Branch developed a product which provides an in-depth description of the foreign investment in the National Industrial Security Program (NISP). The data in this initial document will be used as a baseline for subsequent documents outlining trends in foreign investment in the NISP. The FOCI Analytic Branch also created a process to monitor material changes for facilities in the NISP. These changes are disseminated throughout DSS in a weekly product titled, *FOCI in the News*.

These analytic products allow DSS to move to a proactive, rather than a reactive mode, and allow it to better prepare FOCI mitigation measures in cleared industry.

FOCI best practices

The FOCI Office at DSS Headquarters reviewed and consolidated lessons learned over the last year from several high visibility FOCI cases to increase the effectiveness and efficiency of the process for instituting mitigation agreements, leading to an overall reduction of unmitigated FOCI. For example, by requiring specific information from the company at the beginning of the process, all of DSS will operate from the same company information and there will be fewer inconsistencies to address operationally within DSS.

Industrial Security Letters

DSS issued two Industrial Security Letters (ISLs) during 2009 to clarify National Industrial Security Program (NISP) policy for cleared industry. The first ISL (ISL 2009-01) pertained to the DSS "Manual for the Certification and Accreditation of Classified Systems under the NISP" and the "Standardization of Baseline Technical Security Configurations." The ISL described the baseline safeguards DSS will apply when making an accreditation decision for a contractor information technology system to process classified information.

This ISL is critical to the implementation and adoption of national federal standards for IT systems by cleared industry. Prior to the publication of the ISL, no published baseline standards existed resulting in inconsistent security controls being applied across industry to protect classified information. The ISL clarified confusion that existed among DSS and cleared contractors, and has strengthened DoD's accountability and user access requirements.

The second ISL (ISL 2009-02) addressed three important NISP policy issues. Prior to this ISL, contractors organized and existing in territorial areas other than Puerto Rico were not eligible to be considered for facility clearances. This ISL clarified the eligibility of companies organized and existing under the laws of organized U.S. territorial areas for facility clearances. The policy clarification ensures consistent application of NISP policy in all of the organized U.S. territories.

Additionally, the second ISL establishes consistent application of policy as it applies to potential contractor employees and ensures that DSS is not processing personnel security clearances for individuals who will not begin working right away; and the ISL defined when DSS may invalidate an existing facility clearance if a contractor is unable or unwilling to negotiate an acceptable measure to mitigate foreign ownership, control or influence.

Changing the CI culture

DSS Counterintelligence (CI) is actively engaged in building a "culture of catching spies" not only within DSS, but within the entire cleared defense community. To build that culture, DSS CI is undertaking a number of specific efforts which change the way reporting has been done and refocusing it on the most critical technologies. Central to this effort is ensuring that information available to DSS — including reporting from industry — is effectively triaged, analyzed and referred to the appropriate law enforcement or counterintelligence agency for investigative or operational follow-up. The DSS goal is that any such referrals must be pursued to their logical conclusion.

DSS will build a more effective partnership with industry to ensure they have the knowledge, means and opportunity to report suspicious incidents for timely assessment and appropriate response. The fundamental cultural shift involves changing the prevailing perception within industry (and some government sectors) that reporting a possible unlawful penetration adversely affects how that company's security posture is perceived. To mitigate this perception, DSS will seek to reward those companies that do have effective measures to identify such issues and report them.

This effort will require that DSS CI specialists are available and effectively equipped with the skill-sets and knowledge necessary to assist industry in identifying threats and responding appropriately. The end result will be a CI mindset integrated into all aspects of the DSS mission.

Metrics Report

DSS produces a monthly statistical summary of DoD Personnel Security Investigation (PSI) processing metrics and other elements of the security clearance process. The report includes timeliness metrics, projected vs. actual case volume, DoD pending case inventory levels, and DoD Central Adjudication Facilities' (CAF) adjudication metrics. The report is distributed to the staff of the Under Secretary of Defense for Intelligence, the Military Services and the Defense Agencies as a monthly personnel security program evaluation tool. The assessment tool has been well received and has assisted recipients in tracking actual PSI submissions against budget projections.

... A MORE FUNDAMENTAL CHANGE WE MUST MAKE IN OUR APPROACH TO CYBER SECURITY: WE MUST BE MORE PROACTIVE. WE CAN AND SHOULD DO MORE TO GET AHEAD OF THIS PROBLEM, BUT IT WILL TAKE PARTICIPATION FROM ALL OF THE RELEVANT STAKEHOLDERS, FACILITATED BY STRONG AND CENTRALIZED COORDINATION.

LARRY M. WORTZEL
VICE CHAIRMAN, U.S.-CHINA ECONOMIC AND SECURITY REVIEW COMMISSION

The following initiatives are ongoing at DSS to better meet the needs of the NISP and cleared industry.

Trend analysis

The annual CI publication, *"Targeting U.S. Technology: A Trend Analysis of Reporting from Defense Industry"* analyzes information obtained from suspicious contact reports (SCRs) submitted by industry. This information identifies the most frequently targeted technologies, assesses the most common methods of collection, explores possible motivations and affiliations of those attempting the collection, and identifies the locations where these collection threats originate.

Security officials, cleared contractors, intelligence professionals and DoD policy and decision makers use this information to assess the technology collection threat and develop and implement appropriate measures to mitigate its effect. The most recent version of the document includes a special section on unmanned aerial vehicles (UAV) and the intense interest the technology receives from foreign companies.

Refined Facilities of Interest List

The facilities of interest list (FIL) is a tool designed to rank the more than 13,000 cleared facilities by programs, technologies and level of probable risk, with consideration of the threat at those facilities. The FIL forms the basis of an updated threat mitigation strategy which focuses on technologies most at risk. The FIL is also used to prioritize inspections and tailor the inspection to address the specific threats.

On a quarterly basis, DSS updates the FIL to help focus the efforts of Field CI Specialists and Industry Security Representatives on the protection of DoD's most sensitive technologies. Industrial Security Representatives now indicate the FIL tier level on all suspicious contact reports (SCR) and violation reports concerning facilities in Tiers I and II which contain the most sensitive and critical technologies and facilities. This action helps expedite the SCR process and analysis timeline, and improves the CI feedback to the Industrial Security Representatives and industry on the most critical reporting.

Personnel Security Investigations for Industry (PSI-I) Requirements Survey

In April 2009, DSS deployed its annual web-based survey to 10,953 cleared Industry Facility Security Officers representing 12,189 cleared facilities to project PSI-I requirements. The projections are the key component in Future Years Defense Program (FYDP) DSS/DoD program planning and budgeting for NISP security clearances.

With more than 87.5 percent of cleared contractor facilities responding, representing 94.6 percent of the cleared contractor population, this was the most successful survey to date in terms of industry participation. The survey was conducted using a professional web-based application, which ensures ease of use and standardizes the survey dissemination and data collection process.

	Spring 2009 Survey	Spring 2008 Survey	Fall 2007 Survey	Fall 2006 Survey
Facility Participation Rate	87.5%	83%	70%	51%
Cleared Industry Population Represented	94.6%	92%	83%	61%

The annual survey has proven to be an excellent tool for forecasting industry requirements. At the close of FY09, industry clearance eligibility submissions were 97.6 percent of the 182,315 cases projected through the survey - well within the Office of Management and Budget mandate that the survey results be +/- 5 percent of actual submissions.

Meeting adjudicative timelines

In 2004, Congress enacted the Intelligence Reform and Terrorism Prevention Act (IRTPA). IRTPA mandated specific goals for improving timelines for both personnel security investigations and adjudications. The Defense Industrial Security Clearance Office, the DSS adjudication facility which adjudicates collateral clearances for Industry, continues to exceed the mandated IRTPA guidelines for completion of adjudications.

- In FY09, DISCO completed 90 percent of initial adjudications in 16 days, exceeding the 20-day IRTPA goal.

- DISCO increased the number of interim personnel security clearances granted by 28 percent, from 92,350 in FY08 to 118,323 in FY09.

- DISCO granted 180,166 final personnel security clearances in FY09, as compared to 181,179 in FY08.

ISFO C&A Process Manual

The ISFO Certification and Accreditation Process Manual (formerly the ODAA Process Manual) was revised in 2009. This revision divided the Process Manual into two distinct versions, one specifically for Industry use and one for DSS internal use. The DSS internal version includes all information contained in the Industry version, as well as specific instructions and directions for Information Systems Security Professionals (ISSP) in the field. This helps provide DSS personnel with a 'big picture' of the certification and accreditation process. With the future re-write of NISPOM Chapter 8, the ISFO Process Manual will be an evolving document that will assist DSS in protecting classified information in an ever-changing environment.

The next release of the Process Manual, scheduled for Spring 2010, will provide cleared industry with a desktop reference guide to follow in their compliance responsibilities as well as a training and education tool for new and experienced system security professionals. Most importantly, the Process Manual will address areas of confusion and inconsistency brought to DSS by cleared industry.

> THE NATURE OF THE NATIONAL SECURITY THREAT TO THE U.S. HAS CHANGED OVER TIME. SO IT'S INCUMBENT ON THE INTELLIGENCE COMMUNITY TO NOT ONLY KEEP UP, BUT TO STAY AHEAD OF THE CURVE, AND TO TELL POLICYMAKERS IN WASHINGTON WHERE THAT CURVE IS HEADING.
>
> DENNIS C. BLAIR
> DIRECTOR OF NATIONAL INTELLIGENCE

Expanded training courses

The demand for professional security training continues to grow, and to meet this demand, the SETA expanded its course offerings, seeking news ways to provide training and creating tools to support security education. During the last year, 32 new web-based courses were offered by SETA, including:

- Foreign Disclosure Officer training for the Army (a nine course suite of training)

- Special Adjudication Training for Army contractors

- Physical Security Programs

- Facility Security Officer orientation

- Facility Security Officer management processing

The DSS Academy also expanded its virtual classroom training capability and the Resource Tool for Security Professionals, and provided mobile training delivery of courses critical to the Air Force.

Call Center Operations

The DoD Security Services Call Center is a dual-sited integrated Center (Alexandria, Va., and Columbus, Ohio) that provides front-line user support to the mission systems including:

- The Industrial Security Facilities Database (ISFD) which manages facility information for those cleared contractors participating in the National Industrial Security Program (NISP).
- The Defense Central Index of Investigations (DCII) which allows for the central management and identification of DoD investigative report information.
- The Electronic Network Registration & On-line Learning (ENROL) which is a web-based Learning Management System that automates the administration, documentation, tracking, and reporting of training in support of the Security Education Awareness and Training (SETA) mission area.
- The Electronic Questionnaires for Investigations Processing (e-QIP) system which is part of an e-government initiative sponsored by the U.S. Office of Personnel Management (OPM). e-QIP allows applicants to electronically enter, update, and transmit their personal investigative data over a secure Internet connection to their employing agency for review and approval.

Approximately 1,500 daily callers are supported with a call abandonment rate of less than one percent with an average caller wait time of only seven seconds. In September 2009 part of the Call Center was relocated from the DSS headquarters facility to the Hoffman Building I in Alexandria, Va. with no disruption to service.

AUTOMATION INITIATIVES

During the past year, DSS undertook a number of automation initiatives across the agency to better improve processes and operations.

Electronic transmission of fingerprints

Submission of fingerprints is required to initiate all personnel security investigation requests with the Office of Personnel Management (OPM). Until recently, the process of capturing and submitting a subject's fingerprints was manual, time consuming, and prone to errors. To alleviate these issues, DSS implemented a solution that allows cleared industry to provide fingerprints electronically to OPM.

In November 2007, DSS explored multiple alternatives and selected a CrossMatch Technologies solution that consisted of a store-and-forward server coupled with a custom web application. This system was designated as the Secure Web Fingerprint Transmission system (SWFT).

The SWFT pilot program (SWFT 1.0) began in June 2008. The pilot provided the Initial Operating Capabilities of the system and included four industry partners. Based on the success of the pilot program, DSS developed and implemented an enhanced version of SWFT (SWFT 2.0), allowing full operational capability, and expanded the availability of the system to all cleared industry in July 2009.

During the 14 months of the program, industry participants have uploaded 18,489 electronic fingerprints into the SWFT system, allowing DSS to match and transmit 10,739 of those electronic fingerprints to OPM for further processing.

These voluntary electronic submissions from industry have increased the quality of submissions and reduced the fingerprint rejection rate by approximately nine percent. As of November 2009, 63 Facility Security Officers representing 13 companies have joined the SWFT program and have submitted nearly 11,000 electronic fingerprint files for transmission by the SWFT system to OPM.

While these numbers represent a small piece of the total number of investigative requests, these electronic submissions have eliminated delays associated with mailing paper fingerprint cards. This process has also ensured that fingerprint files were matched to a valid investigation in the Joint Personnel Adjudication System (JPAS) prior to release to OPM.

IN THE 18TH AND 19TH CENTURY WE FACED A THREAT WHERE SHIPS CROSSED THE OCEAN IN DAYS. IN WORLD WAR II, AIRCRAFT COULD CROSS THE OCEAN IN HOURS. IN THE COLD WAR, MISSILES COULD DO IT IN MINUTES. AND NOW TODAY, CYBER ATTACKS CAN STRIKE IN MILLISECONDS.

WILLIAM J. LYNN III
DEPUTY SECRETARY OF DEFENSE

Electronic submission of facility clearances

DSS partnered with the Department of Energy (DOE) to use the DOE electronic FOCI (e-FOCI) submission site to facilitate and enhance DSS' facility clearance and FOCI adjudication and mitigation processes. DSS also worked with DOE to develop a proprietary DSS Electronic Facility Clearance (e-FCL) application, which is scheduled for implementation in early 2010.

The web-based application is designed around the SF 328, "Certificate Pertaining to Foreign Interests," and requires companies to upload and submit their required information into the e-FCL system. This information includes: SF 328, list of key management personnel, list of stockholders, bylaws, and other supporting documentation.

In addition to offering a streamlined and automated process for submission of the SF 328 and supporting documentation, e-FCL enables DSS to process facility clearances more effectively and efficiently while providing a centralized repository to assist in the FOCI adjudication and mitigation process.

Joint Personnel Adjudication System (JPAS) Enhancements

DSS implemented the revised SF-86 (Questionnaire for National Security Positions) in JPAS, allowing DoD to fulfill its commitment nearly two months ahead of its implementation deadline. This enhancement allows cleared industry and military offices to continue processing personnel security clearance requests and smoothly transition to the revised SF-86. DSS implemented interfaces with the Clearance Adjudication Tracking System (CATS) and the Automated Continuing Evaluation System (ACES) to allow critical data to be exchanged in support of DoD Personnel Security reform initiatives. The CATS tool was selected as the DoD non-Intelligence Community IT system / tool for case management and adjudications. The interface allows adjudicative information from CATS to be updated in JPAS, giving security managers visibility into the clearance eligibility status of their personnel. The ACES interface provides JPAS data in support of the ACES automated eligibility assessments conducted between normal investigation cycles.

> IN 1989, WITH THE FALL OF THE BERLIN WALL, THE NATURE OF THREATS AGAINST US BECAME A LOT LESS CLEAR CUT, AND MUCH MORE COMPLEX. AND THEN IN SEPTEMBER 2001, EVERYTHING CHANGED AGAIN. THE CHALLENGE FOR TODAY'S INTELLIGENCE COMMUNITY IS: NOW WE NEED TO WORRY NOT ONLY ABOUT THE OLD STANDARDS OF NUCLEAR MISSILES, INSURGENCIES, AND SPIES FROM OTHER NATIONS, BUT OTHER GLOBAL THREATS. AND POWERFUL, DANGEROUS ORGANIZATIONS THAT ARE NOT NATIONS.
>
> DENNIS C. BLAIR
> DIRECTOR OF NATIONAL INTELLIGENCE

JPAS Certification and Accreditation

DSS certified and accredited JPAS by validating the security controls, and obtained an Authority to Operate on the Nonsecure Internet Protocol Router Network (NIPRNet). DSS complied with various Defense Information Systems Agency, Joint Task Force-Global Network Operations security vulnerability alerts and tested all patches and upgrades to ensure requirements were implemented and new problems were not introduced into the system. DSS responded and provided resolution to various JPAS incidents involving government and contract personnel. In addition, DSS initiated a network security solution which provides real-time analysis of network flows and models behavior to identify abnormal activity. DSS installed U. S. Army Research Laboratory sensors to monitor external traffic between routers and firewalls for abnormal activity on the DSS unclassified data network.

> GOVERNMENTS OF ALL STRIPES SEEM TO HAVE GREAT DIFFICULTY SUMMONING THE WILL AND THE RESOURCES TO DEAL EVEN WITH THREATS THAT ARE OBVIOUS AND LIKELY INEVITABLE, MUCH LESS THREATS THAT ARE MORE COMPLEX OR OVER THE HORIZON.
>
> ROBERT M. GATES
> SECRETARY OF DEFENSE

During the past year, DSS has launched an agency-wide campaign to reach out to the larger security, counterintelligence and stakeholder communities to share information and establish face-to-face working relationships.

Security Manager's Forum

The Security Education, Training and Awareness (SETA) Directorate planned and conducted the 2009 Security Managers' Forum, which was attended by more than 200 civilian and military security professionals. The forum included senior representatives from the Office of the Under Secretary of Defense for Intelligence who addressed policy changes, on-going initiatives and related topics of interest affecting the DoD security environment. The highlight of the forum, however, was an FBI presentation of the Chi Mak espionage investigation. The presentation was provided by an FBI Special Agent with first-hand knowledge of this highly publicized case.

To increase access to the event, a live Webcast of the proceedings was provided to those who couldn't attend in person. This outreach and awareness initiative promotes the exchange of information and highlights initiatives that impact the DoD military, civilian and contractor communities across the security disciplines.

Stakeholder Board

The Defense Security Service Stakeholder Board was established in February 2009 to provide a forum for consultation and the sharing of information among Department of Defense components and offices on matters related to industrial security and DSS operations. The board held three meetings in FY09 and the agendas focused on a number of issues of interest to members, such as cyber security, DSS actions to address results of the Personnel Security Investigations for Industry (PSI-I) Requirements Survey, and the PSI costs in industry.

The format is designed to elicit open discussion of issues pertinent to DSS and the larger security community. The Board is an advisory and not a decision making body, and is not established to preclude other communications among the Board members. It serves as a primary means of communication for DSS and a forum to raise issues of mutual concern within the Department.

Industry Stakeholders

DSS held a meeting of Industry Stakeholders as part of an active effort to meet on a recurring basis with representatives from industry to discuss issues of mutual interest and concern. The Industry group is comprised of representatives from the various industry associations, the industry representatives to the National Industrial Security Program Policy Advisory Committee, and corporate security officials from the largest cleared contractors. The first meeting allowed for a free exchange of concerns and focused on upcoming DSS initiatives and how they would affect industry.

DoD Security Training Council (DSTC)

The Director, DSS is designated by DoD Instruction 3305.13 as the functional manager responsible for the execution and maintenance of DoD security training. In this capacity, the Director is responsible for establishing the DoD Security Training Council (DSTC). The DSTC is an advisory body on DoD security training, which is comprised of appointed representatives from the DoD components.

The DSTC was formally established on Oct. 15, 2008, and since its establishment, the DSTC has driven the professionalization of the security workforce by developing skill sets and criteria. The DSTC has reviewed current security skill standards, updated and validated those standards, and reviewed component comments on the current draft certification model and the development schedule for the DoD security certification program.

Professionalization of the security workforce meets the DoD objective of providing an official and standardized framework for security professionals to identify and receive required training and ultimately achieve a security certification credential.

Government Industrial Security Working Group (GISWG)

The purpose of the GISWG is to provide a forum for sharing information between DSS and the Government Agencies for which it provides industrial security services under the National Industrial Security Program (NISP). The group meets two to three times per year and the agenda focuses on topic areas that are of particular interest to the Government Agencies due to new policies or procedures or those that require clarification.

Building an effective Insider Threat program

Cleared industry is home to some of the United States' most critical and sensitive information. Counterintelligence and security specialists believe that the greatest threat to the integrity, confidentiality and accessibility of this information in industry is the "insider threat." The term "insider threat" refers to someone with legitimate access to sensitive information, who takes malicious actions with that information.

The risk of insider attacks is greatest for systems that contain high value, mission critical data. These high value targets may be classified or unclassified government systems or systems in the private sector.

The DSS Insider Threat program is focused on enhancing training and awareness throughout industry and includes provisions to encourage industry reporting and the need to follow through on recommendations. DSS CI is exploring a new computer-based "threat awareness training" platform that will enable DSS to reach hundreds of cleared contractors quickly and efficiently.

Transition of legacy IT systems

The Deputy Secretary of Defense directed DSS to transfer "DoD enterprise wide IT systems associated with personnel security clearances to the Defense Manpower Data Center." These systems include the Joint Personnel Adjudication System (JPAS); the Defense Central Index of Investigations (DCII); the Secure Web Fingerprint Transmission (SWFT); and, the Investigative Records Repository (IRR).

DSS and DMDC have met regularly over the past year to ensure a smooth technical transition of the systems and to ensure the transfer is transparent with no interruption in service.

> IT'S BEEN SAID THAT "TRYING TO PREDICT THE FUTURE IS LIKE TRYING TO DRIVE DOWN A COUNTRY ROAD AT NIGHT WITH NO LIGHTS, WHILE LOOKING OUT THE BACK WINDOW." BUT THAT'S EXACTLY WHAT WE HAVE TO DO IN THE U.S. INTELLIGENCE COMMUNITY.
>
> DENNIS C. BLAIR
> DIRECTOR OF NATIONAL INTELLIGENCE

Next Generation Automation

DSS is developing the next generation Industrial Security automation tools to support the growing industrial facility security, counterintelligence, training and headquarters mission areas. Significant development efforts will include a Business Management System that will manage the submission and processing of System Security Plans (SSPs). An Electronic Facilities Clearance system will manage facility information for those cleared contractors participating in the National Industrial Security Program (NISP), to include any information pertaining to a facility's foreign ownership, control, or influence. A DD 254 Database will allow the tracking of all contractor security classification specifications awarded to cleared facilities. A CI Analytical Automation System will provide advanced collection, analysis, and reporting capabilities. The DSS Chief Information Officer is looking at a Service Oriented Architecture (Reusable enterprise services) that allows major capabilities to be deployed as interoperable services and promotes capability reuse as well as Identity Management (single sign-on) to provide users with role-based access to DSS Mission Systems. Finally, the new automation will provide a Secure Portal – a secure point of entry into the automated information and missions critical systems.

CASE STUDIES

The following case studies provide lessons learned for DSS, the cleared defense community and Government Contracting Activities.

Counterintelligence: Industry reporting safeguards sensitive technology

In April 2008, a suspicious individual sent a direct request email to a cleared defense contractor, asking the contractor to add the individual as a friend on a popular social networking site. After establishing contact, the suspicious individual emailed the contractor again asking to purchase launch systems technology, a subset of the Developing Science and Technologies List's armaments and energetic materials technology. In keeping with the requirements in the National Industrial Security Program Operating Manual, the cleared facility reported the incidents to DSS.

A review of DSS and all-source intelligence community reporting revealed that this was not the individual's first attempt to obtain controlled or restricted technology. In 1989, the U.S. Customs Service investigated and arrested the individual for attempting to export ammunition, TOW missiles, and 500 units of sarin nerve gas to Iran. The culprit was convicted and sentenced to 30 months in prison for those 1989 crimes. Further industry reporting revealed that, in May 2007, the same individual sent a series of direct request emails to multiple cleared facilities requesting information on various missile technologies. In that instance as well, the cleared facility ended all contact with the suspicious person and referred the case to DSS CI.

Immigrations and Customs Enforcement (ICE) opened an investigation on the individual in September 2008. The investigating officer established contact with the individual, and the individual sent him a friend request to join the social networking site. Once contact was established, the individual asked the undercover investigator for satellite launch and rocket propellant technology. The investigation continued and on April 15, 2009, ICE agents arrested the subject in Florida for attempting to sell missile launch technology to Russia. The individual was charged with violations against the Arms Export Control Act, the Missile Technology Control regime and the International Trafficking in Arms Regulations.

> **This is a prime example of the importance of industry reporting. Reporting suspicious contacts of this nature to DSS CI can identify unlawful penetration attempts to the cleared defense industrial base. With this reporting, DSS CI can aid local or national law enforcement to exploit or neutralize a foreign intelligence element or criminal agent.**

String of stolen laptops

During a security review, DSS found that several laptops, containing unclassified information, had been stolen from a cleared facility. The theft was reported by the Industrial Security Specialist (ISS) to the Field Counterintelligence Specialist (FCIS) in the local DSS field office. The FCIS wrote a report and shared concerns with local law enforcement offices about the growing trend, and asked to be notified if any other cleared facilities in the area had property stolen. The report was discussed at a local Counterintelligence Working Group in which the FBI took interest. The local FBI office discovered a possible relationship to persons of interest and joined the effort, and later established a task force to address this issue. One of the first efforts of this task force was to release a Law Enforcement Bulletin within a large geographic area to alert other local law enforcement to this pattern of theft. The task force continues to monitor laptop thefts and provides feedback to DSS along with requests for information about cleared contractor facilities.

> **DSS actions in this office led to an improved relationship with the law enforcement community and ultimately to recognition of an activity that may have an impact on National Security. DSS continues to support this effort with both statistical and analytical information.**

FOCI mitigation

A large cleared research facility notified DSS in January 2009 of the appointment of a foreign citizen as President with an effective date in less than two months from the notification. The facility, along with a research lab as a division, is one of the largest cleared facilities in the United States.

Under the National Industrial Security Program Operational Manual, paragraph 2-104, both the senior management official and the facility security officer must always be cleared to the level of the facility clearance, and only U.S. citizens are eligible for a personnel security clearance. Appointment of a non-U.S. citizen as the senior management official renders a company ineligible for a facility clearance and puts the company under foreign ownership, control, or influence (FOCI).

To assist the company in retaining its facility clearance, DSS offered the facility FOCI mitigation. The facility decided to amend its by-laws to remove the President's authority to perform duties as a senior management official. However, none of the proposed changes removed or changed the authority vested in the President. DSS informed the facility that if it did not present a viable plan prior to the non-U.S. citizen taking office, then DSS would invalidate the facility clearance.

The facility opted to use another mitigation strategy and notified DSS that they would form a separate legal entity for the purpose of performing the facility's classified contracts. DSS approved the plan and did not invalidate the facility clearance.

DSS has the flexibility and tools to analyze and, when possible, mitigate foreign influence on any business structure. Companies should involve DSS early in the process to ensure valuable time and resources are not wasted.

Classified Material Found in Home

A former cleared employee of a cleared facility was found dead in his residence in June 2009. Shortly after his death, the family discovered classified information at the decedent's home with five boxes of classified information ultimately recovered. DSS conducted an Administrative Inquiry (AI) and interviewed current and former company employees. An additional 40 to 50 boxes of mixed unclassified, For Official Use Only, company proprietary, and classified (Confidential and Secret) material were found at the residence. DSS concluded that most of the classified material discovered at the residence originated from a cleared facility and branch office.

An unannounced security inspection of the cleared facility confirmed that some of their classified holdings matched those discovered at the decedent's residence. The DSS inquiry determined that at least three employees of the cleared facility received phone calls from three different individuals, while the deceased employee was alive, reporting that he had classified information in his possession. Further inquiry disclosed that the deceased had been terminated from employment in September 2006 due to alcohol abuse, work performance, and personal conduct issues; none of which were reported to DSS. The unannounced inspection revealed additional serious findings at the facility to include a failure to report adverse/suspicious information, operating an unaccredited classified information system, and retaining classified information without proper authority. An Unsatisfactory security rating was issued to the facility and a compliance inspection scheduled.

Interview of employee personnel using in-depth and probing questions during DSS inspections is critical to developing potential security issues. If the facility's security personnel had properly interviewed their internal employee at the time the adverse information incidents were occurring and/or shortly after the allegations of improper possession of classified were made, it is highly probable that this security violation would have come to the attention of DSS much sooner.

Who should investigate?

During a certification visit for an IT system, the DSS representative overheard some employees discussing the recent firing of several other employees and allegations involving the piracy of media. The DSS representative recognized the names of at least two of the employees who were fired as personnel who were cleared and performed functions as System Administrators on some of the accredited information systems at the facility.

When the DSS representative questioned the facility personnel about the matter, the facility personnel refused to comment as the matter was under investigation by the facility's Corporate Ethics Office. When asked if the Corporate Security Office was aware of the investigation, the management official was unable to answer. He did indicate however, that at least five cleared personnel had been fired for alleged misuse of company assets/equipment. He also alleged that the personnel were "running some sort of side business" and using company equipment/assets to run this business.

No adverse information reports had been submitted on any of the individuals cited. The local DSS office launched an administrative inquiry into the matter which determined that no classified systems were involved. However, the inquiry also revealed that eight employees of either the facility or another cleared division were terminated for varying degrees of participation in the file sharing of copyrighted movies, music and software using company owned unclassified computer assets. Five additional employees who were either facility employees or employees of another cleared division, were alleged to have known about the situation but did not report it and were suspended and reprimanded.

The inquiry determined that there appeared to be a breakdown between the facility's security, human resource and ethics offices over reporting requirements. As a result of the inquiry, adverse information reports were submitted for the 13 cleared employees involved in the initial allegations of copyright violations. A member of the security department is now a member of the facility's Administrative Review Committee for all employee incidents, not just incidents that involve a classified asset. The facility also modified its policy to invite participation of a representative from the security staff at any discussion/review of disciplinary cases, regardless of behavior or conduct under investigation, where the alleged violator has or is in-process for a Personnel Security Clearance (PCL). Facility management also agreed to ensure appropriate notification is made to the security office when an employee who has, or is in the process of getting, a PCL is being terminated (voluntary or involuntary).

Finally, the corporation has a Computer Information Response Team (CIRT) which has representatives assigned at each entity throughout the corporation. Previously, the CIRT representatives did not work in conjunction with the local security offices. The CIRT representatives would work with members of the Corporate Ethics Office when assisting in the conduct of Ethics Investigations involving personnel who were alleged to have been misusing the unaccredited corporate computer systems. Since the AI pertained to adverse information associated with misuse of an unaccredited corporate computer system, along with other allegations, the Corporate Security Office has worked with the Corporate Ethics Office, to ensure that CIRT representatives keep the local security offices informed if a cleared individual is involved in any way with regard to an investigation being handled by a local CIRT representative.

The event resulted in a much closer relationship between the Corporate Security Office and the Corporate Ethics Office as well as better communication between the local security offices and the local ethics offices at each of the cleared corporate entities, and better communication between DSS and the facility.

> **The Administrative Inquiry revealed a breakdown at the facility with regard to the reporting of Adverse Information associated with ethics investigations initiated by the Corporate Ethics Office. The case also revealed a similar weakness throughout the entire corporation.**

DSS PRIORITIES AND PREPARING FOR THE FUTURE

For the coming year, DSS will continue to enhance and expand the National Industrial Security Program and reinvigorate the Security Education, Training and Awareness Program. Our priorities are:

Computer-based training for industry

Under the new focus of identifying unlawful penetrators, computer-based training will be one method to spread the word to industry about the reality of the threat and steps they can take to mitigate the threat. The goal is to launch this program within a year.

Industrial awards recognition program

DSS Counterintelligence is taking a new approach to reward cleared companies for uncovering unlawful penetrators. The premise for establishing the awards program is the reality that every company has, or likely will be, unlawfully penetrated, and as such, reporting these actors will no longer have negative connotations. Instead, DSS will track and reward the top 10 facilities with the highest number of unlawful penetrators reported, and the highest number of facility personnel who have completed the DSS threat awareness training programs. DSS will, in turn, positively promote those facilities which have excelled in this competition.

FOCI

DSS is leveraging best practices to refine FOCI requirements for industry and ensure that the FOCI compliance framework is geared toward the FOCI risks, which continue to evolve. DSS has consolidated lessons learned from previous cases and will in coming months issue updated policies and mitigation templates which are coordinated with operational requirements. FOCI Action Officers have reduced response times by one-third, which allows a more proactive approach to FOCI issues.

Training

SETA is constantly searching out innovative methods to deliver training and increase the scope of the training offered. Currently, there are more than 30 courses in development, which includes building a curriculum for accreditation of the DSS work force.

Automation

DSS is realigning its contractor and civilian Information Technology (IT) resources to better support field operations. Projected improvements include a government project manager for each region, additional telecommunications engineers and regional contract support technicians who can travel to support remote offices. Delivering high quality IT support to all DSS locations will result in a more effective, efficient workforce and allow DSS field personnel to focus on their counterintelligence and industrial security missions.

Preparing for the future

While proud of our successes, DSS continuously seeks to improve its performance as the premier provider of personnel and industrial security services in the Department of Defense (DoD). Through new ideas, innovations and expanded technology, DSS will continue to ensure the security of our nation and our warfighters.

> ...WE HAVE TO BE VIGILANT IN DEFENDING OUR PEOPLE AT HOME. AND THAT TAKES AGGRESSIVE INTELLIGENCE COLLECTION AND SKILLFUL ANALYSIS. AND THAT DEMANDS THE EFFECTIVE AND EFFICIENT COORDINATION BETWEEN FEDERAL GOVERNMENT AND OUR STATE AND LOCAL PARTNERS.
>
> BARACK H. OBAMA
> PRESIDENT OF THE UNITED STATES